AIR COMMAND AND STAFF COLLEGE

AIR UNIVERSITY

AMERICA'S WAR ON TERROR: ISLAMIC JIHADIST IDEOLOGUE OR RADICAL

HIJACKER OF ISLAM – WILL THE REAL ENEMY PLEASE STEP FORWARD

by

Patrick Martin Miller, Major, USAF

i

Contents

Preface

Of the many things presented at Air Command and Staff College, one key take-away is the contention, as unfortunate at times as it may be, that we, either as a nation, a military institution, a service, or even as an individual tend to see things as we expect them to be. We also avoid things that are uncomfortable and likely difficult to address; and, we see things in light of our own interests. The Arab Culture elective, both course instructors and texts, afforded me a great opportunity to look behind the curtain of my personal biases and attempt a more holistic view of the world, more specifically the current global conflict America and the Western world finds itself amidst, thus the impetus behind this topic.

With this said, the research method used for this paper is the problem/solution. The problem examined focuses on the relationship between Islam and the militant, Jihad ideology in which ends are justified by the means. This paper explores a current perceived shortcoming in the United States' National Security Strategy (NSS) as it looks to confront the before-mentioned ideology and offers alternative methods that might more effectively counter the associated terrorists and aid in winning the hearts and minds of the "moderate" Muslim populace.

Lastly, although the key contention with this paper rests on the premise that American NSS is flawed due to separating the terrorist from his/her religion (Islam), the intent is not to be aligned with any attempted critique of the religion – such is completely outside the scope of this discussion. With this said, the bottom-line objective is to substantiate the premise that since you cannot separate the jihadist from his/her belief, it only appears logical that you would be unable to mitigate these terrorists' effects without a strategy that took both the individual and the individual's religion into account. Therefore, this paper seeks to explore this relationship.

Abstract

The United States National Security Strategy contends that the War on Terror is a "battle of ideas – a fight against the terrorists and against their murderous ideology." In turn, it separates the radical Islamist from their religion - Islam. The problem with this contention rests with the fact that there is no separation of religion from the terrorists', nor from their murderous ideology. In light of this disconnect, a new comprehensive counter strategy is required. Furthermore, ascribing to the premise that today's fight represents a global insurgency, the revised strategy must seek out ways to employ America's and its allies' full complement of instruments of national power. These efforts could be used to aid a grassroots establishment of a non-Western, moderate Islamic voice, go on an offensive information operations campaign, or even foster the development of a new form of Pan-Arabism. The end goal would be to create a unifying counter ideological effort and win the hearts and minds of the moderate Muslim community. By winning over the hearts and minds of this populace, the counterinsurgency would gain the upper hand over the effectiveness of the insurgent's efforts and his ability to use the population for his ends, and eventually achieve victory.

Introduction

James Joule, the 19th Century English physicist, first demonstrated the law of conservation of energy contending that energy in an isolated system can neither be created nor destroyed. However, what can transpire within such a system is for the energy to change from one form to another.[1] The relevance of this maxim of physics to this paper and America's War on Terror ties to the assumption that the nature of the international system the United States (U.S.) and the other global players of today find themselves amidst, a two-front war, both near and far, with an adversary bent on the destruction of the Western worldview, is the same system that presented itself in Arabia and its surrounding regions almost 1400-plus years ago. And, like the before stated law, while the system has not changed, nor the nature of conflict transpiring within it, what has evolved over this period of time is the conflict's character relative to how society sees, accepts, and articulates, the detriment of the conflict to the system. In summation, it is the combination of this static nature of conflict and the need to revise strategy to account for the change in its character that serves as the impetus of this paper. And, although bleak in many regards, it is believed that appropriate solutions are available; they simply need to be brought forward and accepted by today's leaders. For this assumption aligns with the words of the well known British military theorist and commentator, J.F.C. Fuller who stated, "The main difficulty [in problem solving] has nearly always lain not in the solution itself, but in the acceptance of the solution by those who have a vested interest in the existing methods."[2] Moreover, society today must choose a solution that is more than just palatable and self-serving, for a solution-set based on the empirical evidence of the situation is required.

Using this analogy as a springboard into the heart of the matter, the discussion begins with the current National Security Strategy (NSS) document which opens with a letter from former

President George W. Bush stating "America is at war."[3] The document goes on to outline the way ahead in this War on Terror and articulates that it is a "battle of ideas – a fight against the terrorists and against their murderous ideology."[4] The problem with this machination resides in the reality that there is little, if any, separation of religion and state in the Islamic world. Furthermore, there is no separation of religion from the terrorists' murderous ideology. For the radical Islamist, their struggle or jihad is centrally a spiritual one and is seen by means which are justified by the ends they pursue – the establishment of a world-wide, pan-Islamic religious state/system or Caliphate.[5] Accordingly, to deny this relationship, would be to deny that the jihadist terrorism, which the world experiences daily, is in fact born of religion – Sharia-driven Islam.[6] Therefore, in using the initial analogy, the ideology and those who pursue its militant ends are of the same mold as those from Islam's inception. Their reach is now just more expansive and the characteristics of war more advanced, but the means to their ends are alike.

For America to defeat this foe, it must more effectively confront the reality of today's conflict. It must recognize the critical flaw in its strategy, that being the failure to acknowledge religion, Islam, as the central "cause" behind the enemy's actions, as well as being their source of strength and power. Furthermore, the visage of political correctness, in which all non-, overtly terroristic Muslims are moderates, must be cast aside. By doing so, this fight can start being addressed for what it is, a conflict between "incompatible value systems (Western/Democratic versus Muslim/Sharia) having different cosmological assumptions about the proper relationship of individual human beings to those governing them…"[7] This means America must step outside the Western, secular-Democratic mind-set and begin listening to the words and, in turn, the nefarious intentions, today's jihadists' have been so clearly articulating to the "free" world. These intentions center on the objective of destroying the entire

2

Western/secular community and the implementation of a global Islamic state. It is from this vantage point that an American counter offensive must begin. Unless the U.S. confronts this reality it will never adequately be able to address and develop strategies that feed from the fact that Islam has over 1,400 years of tradition which serves as the basis for its political-cultural-religious organizing principle. And, unless we begin to understand this tradition and acknowledge the critical role religion plays in it, what has been deemed the long war may just become the lost war.

With all this said, the bottom-line upfront intent of this paper is to argue the contention that American strategy to confront radical Islamic terrorists must do battle against both a people and a religion. As such, the problem examined focuses on the relationship between Arab traditions, political-cultural-religious – as it relates to jihadist ideology in which the ends are justified by the means. Furthermore, in setting such as an American objective to national security, an alternative course of action for victory will be offered by exploring the current perceived shortcoming with stated U.S. National Security Strategy and look at how a change in this strategy may more effectively posture the country for accomplishing its stated ends – the guarantee of the Western way of life as a free and open society and an intolerance to violent extremists and all who support them[8] - will also be addressed. To make this case, the discussion begins with a development of the historical context of Islam, particularly Muhammad and the initial spread of his message. This message is then expounded on and an articulation of the two forms of jihadist ideology and their expression is relayed. From this expression, the paper transitions to a look at the nature of today's fight, then concludes with a number of recommended changes to said course of action along with an accompanied way ahead.

In advance of moving any further into the discussion, it is important to note that throughout the document there will be "hesitations" used to offer clarification to critical terminology. The intent is to insure an accurate context is developed for the reader. However, along with the usage of the various key words and associated meanings, a realization to the fact that the greater focus is not the word itself, but the intended usage of the word. For impact will certainly be lost to the reader if mired down by semantics. With this caution flagged, the following series of words are defined upfront, for they will be referenced throughout the document and serve as linchpins for the acceptance of the premise that American strategy for the War on Terror must not/cannot separate the religion, Islam, from those that adhere to it and, whether perversely or not, and, in turn, must adopt counter measures that aligns accordingly.

The first of these terms is radical, which is intended to describe an individual or individuals who favor extreme or revolutionary changes. In the context of this discussion these changes refer to the destruction of the Western world through the waging of *jihad*, or effort made to further Islam through violent means, and the establishment of a *caliphate* or world-wide government representing the political unity and leadership of the Muslim community or *umma*.[9] Likewise, the term militant describes those who advocate such violence to achieve their desired ends. Additionally there is Islamism that refers to the ideology which promotes political control of the state according to the principles of Islam and Islamic law (*sharia*). Stated another way, an Islamist advocates Islam as the constitution for political rule.[10] Lastly is the word terrorist, which represents an individual who employs terrorism to achieve a desired effect, with terrorism being defined as "premeditated, politically motivated violence perpetrated against non-combatant targets by sub-national groups or clandestine agents usually intended to influence an audience."[11] Supplementing this description it must be noted that the influence mentioned is typically through fear and the motivation also includes religious and ideological goals in addition to just political ones.

Historical Context of Conflict

Keeping these terms in mind, the next several points of discussion provide the historical context of Islam, the man who would become its messenger, Muhammad, and the attempts at its propagation through jihad. Starting with the religion, *Islam* is an Arabic word that means submission, with God or *Allah* being the deistic entity worshipers (*Muslims*) submit themselves to. For someone to become a Muslim, the would-be follower is expected to make a sincere profession of faith. The impetus of this statement is that there is no god but God and that Muhammad is God's messenger. As such, all rules of belief and conduct are a result of God's direction given to Muhammad.[12]

Islam traces its origin to the early part of the seventh century A.D. when a man named Muhammad is reportedly visited by Gabriel, an angel of God. The ensuing conversation between the two resulted in the communication of God's will and commandments to the world. This dialogue is believed to be God's final message to humanity and, as recorded, has become known as the *Qur'an* or Islam's holy book, which is "the fundamental, immutable source of Islamic doctrine and practice."[13] While the Qur'an serves as the highest authority to Muslims, being that it was directly given by Allah, Muslims also abide by a collection of sayings and examples from the life of Muhammad. These sayings are recorded in the *Hadith*. The latter's significance is that Muhammad's life reflects the "highest ideal" and "perfect example" which serves to provide Muslims with a source of motivation and direction.[14]

As the historical account further relays, Muhammad communicated this message with his family and close associates, but over the course of time attempted to broaden his base and share his faith with others living in his home town of Mecca, located in the western part of Saudi Arabia. It is important to note, that at the time of receipt of Allah's word, Mecca was a very pagan-oriented town controlled by a non-religious group of leaders. These leaders came to view Muhammad and the monotheistic message he was sharing as a threat to their polytheistic way of life. As Muhammad's efforts to convert the peoples of Mecca increased so did the persecution levied against him by its rulers. This eventually led to Muhammad's decision to leave Mecca and move approximately 150 miles north to the town of Medina, also in Saudi Arabia. Medina's inhabitants were a compilation of pagan Arabs and Jewish tribes. The importance of this journey or *hijira* is that it is looked upon as the beginning of Muslim history and the starting date for the Islamic calendar.[15]

Over the initial several years of Muhammad's stay in Medina, he successfully won the Arab tribesman over to the new religion; however, his efforts at proselytization fell short with the Jews, for as Caner contends, "The Jews noticed the contradictions between the Hebrew Scriptures and the Qur'an and rejected Muhammad's message and authority."[16] This difference of scriptural interpretation serves as the seminal point of contention between not only the Jews and Muslims at the time, but also eventually between Muslims and Christians. For Islam and its message, as relayed in the Qur'an, is not new or original. In fact, Muslims believe that God gave the Jews and the Christians His word in advance to the Muslims; however, to a Muslim, the former perverted it over time. This professed perversion thus precipitated the need for God to send Gabriel to Muhammad to give the world His message once and for all. As such, for a Muslim, the Qur'an is the true, inerrant, and uncorrupted version of God's word to man.[17]

Carrying this premise further, another associated Islamic tenant expresses the supremacy of Allah's will and the fact that Allah has the final say so on the destiny of all. Along this vein, no human is guaranteed Allah's favor, to include Muhammad, and, in turn, not promised paradise. "There is no security for the believer of Islam....The question of whether one is admitted to heaven is left unanswered until the Day of Judgment."[18] The distinction to be made of this is a resultant works-based mentality in which a believer attempts to earn salvation through his/her good works as expressed in *surah* (chapter:verse) 3:24 which states, "But how will it be, when We gather them for a day whereon is no doubt, and every soul shall be paid in full what it has earned, and they shall not be wronged."[19] The end-all for this sentiment resounds in the expression from surah 3:194 "those who suffered hurt in My way, and fought, and were slain – them I shall surely acquit of their evil deeds, and I shall admit them to gardens underneath which rivers flow."[20] The relevance of these texts is that they tie to a believer's hope that if he/she gives their life for "the cause" their evil deeds will be forgiven and paradise will be gained; a key enabler when associated with the mandate to spread the word, particularly through the use violence, as will be discussed next.

This justification of action and seemingly guaranteed ticket to paradise solidifies the militancy witnessed between believers and non-believers. This divide is expressed through *surah* 9:29 in the Qur'an which states, "Fight those who believe not in God and the Last Day and do not forbid what God and His messenger have forbidden – such men as practice not the religion of truth, being of those who have been given the book [Jews and Christians] - until they pay the tribute [*jizya* or alms tax] out of hand and have been humbled."[21] It is from this directive to fight those who resist the submission to Allah that ground zero for today's conflict between militant Islamists and all others emanates. This drive to spread the message through force gives witness to the militancy of not only the messenger, but also the message and serves as a key maxim to the believer as they seek to follow in Muhammad's footsteps spreading God's revelation. Therefore, for the purposes of this paper, this struggle to advance Islam through the waging of jihad represents an "ordinance of Allah essential for the continuation of the Muslim community."[22] Accordingly, the jihadists' effort revolves around the continuation of this militant expansion until the whole world finally accepts Allah as the one true God and is to "be achieved by extending the authority and also the membership of the community which embraces the true faith by upholding God's law."[23] Therefore, jihad presents itself as a clear, simple edict – convert, be conquered, or be killed.

In this context, it is posited that jihad arose. In fact, it follows these lines that Muhammad spent the last several years of his life pursuing a series of battles to increase Islam's base and expand its reach through violent territorial expansion serving not only as Islam's prophet, but also as its warrior. As Cook contends, the associated evidence of these actions reflect the significance of jihad to the early Muslim community.[24] Additionally, based on the presumption that they were fought according to the direction of Allah, the perpetrators found religious justification for their actions. Craner argues this justification finds added emphasis through announced incentives for those who fight Allah's cause as depicted in surah 4:96, "Unto all [in faith] has Allah promised good: But those who strive and fight has He distinguished above those who sit [at home] by a great reward."[25] Following suit, two additional points of reference for these militant enterprises find expressions in surahs 2:212 and 9:5. The former denotes, "Prescribed for you is fighting…,"[26] while the latter directs followers to "…slay the idolaters wherever you find them, and take them, and confine them, and lie in wait for them at every place of ambush. But if they repent, and perform the prayer, and pay the alms, then let them go their way…"[27] As expressed, the "Qur'an presents a well-developed religious justification for waging war against Islam's enemies."[28]

Whereupon, these few examples provide a clear representation of the militant sentiment interwoven within Muhammad's message, they also offer support to the pretense of the divine mandate to exercise jihad in compliance to Islamic tenants put forth by Allah. Articulated slightly differently, "The ideas supported by the jihadis did not spring from a void, nor are all of them the marginal opinions of a few fanatics. The principle dogmas that they assert have [deep] roots in discussions about Islamic law and theology…"[29] Therefore, the bottom-line finding is one of acceptance by the subscriber to such a cause and belief in the use of militant means which finds justification through their ends. Asserting such an ascription, it must be added that this position does not contend that all Muslims are jihadists; however, it does relay that all jihadists are Muslims and both groups find relationship through a closely knit base of belief - Islam. However, the main difference between jihadis and other Muslims focuses on the extremists' commitment to the violent overthrow of the existing international system and its replacement by an all encompassing Islamic state[30] where the latter displays an outward commitment to the employment of more peaceful actions. Accordingly, the resultant schism in orthodoxy based on the use of violence serves as the central theme of the next topic – offensive, lesser jihad versus defensive, greater jihad.

Jihadist Ideology

Looking at the defensive or greater jihad first, it is often accorded the meaning of "struggle." In a general sense, this type of jihad can be broken down into three parts, with the first two tied to the Muslim community, while the third is associated with non-Muslims. Regarding the former, the first aspect of greater jihad is that of the individual who struggles against him/herself in the attainment of purity.[31] It is a struggle against self, an effort to be a better person. The second form, also internal to the Muslim community associates with the concept of spreading Islam to the world, but via peaceful means, through *dawah*, or "the call."[32] The last of the three forms of greater jihad focuses on a struggle between believers and non-believers. The crux of this form lies in the perception that the non-believer is oppressing or hindering the acceptance of Islam. In turn, the Muslim is placed in a defensive position in which they must forcefully respond to satisfy the mandates of Allah as stated in surahs 2:187 and 2:190 which read respectively, "And fight in the way of God with those who fight with you...,"[33] and, "...Whoso commits aggression against you, do you commit aggression against him, like as he has committed against you..."[34] From this position Habeck proposes that jihad was never meant to be associated with warfare for the sake of national or personal gain, but rather a struggle for the sake of Allah.[35]

Extending this sentiment further, jihad means utmost effort in promotion and defense of Islam, which might or might not include armed conflict with unbelievers.[36] Using this perspective as base, it is contended by proponents of greater jihad that this defensive form is exactly what Muhammad employed against the inhabitants of Arabia as he struggled to reveal God's word and lead them out of ignorance (*jahiliyya*). Another example would be the renowned military general Saladin who receives credit for mobilizing Muslims to defeat European Crusaders. In these examples, this defensive type of jihad connotes not a holy type of war, but one that is just in the sense of freeing people from falsehood and oppression.[37] In spite of the seemingly sound case made by proponents of greater jihad, there is an extant divide between such theory and the practice of the second form of jihad termed lesser or offensive, which the discussion now turns to.

In order to best understand the impetus behind the lesser or offensive form of jihad, it is critical to recall back to the previously discussed goal for all Muslims, the establishment of a world-wide Islamic state. This end state fosters the extreme motivation for the offensive-minded jihadist to find religious justification for their actions as they obey Allah's commands to make his word supreme while opening Islam to all nations, thus making the caliphate the leader of the world.[38] Accordingly, it is to this sacred duty that these jihadists find cause, while it is from within the Muslims' holy texts that they find the basis for their action(s). Accordingly, as Lewis states, "For most of the recorded history of Islam, from the lifetime of the Prophet Muhammad onward, the word jihad was used in a primarily military sense."[39] An example of this as argued by Cook is expressed by the fact that the word jihad, used to describe fighting appears in surahs 9:24 and 60:1. Cook goes on to add that when referencing the root or verbal derivatives of the word, jihad appears over and over again with regard to fighting and offers the following references from the Qur'an as examples of such a case: 2:218, 3:143, 8:72, 74-75, 9:16, 20, 41, 86, and 61:11.[40] Supplementing this assertion, Gabriel maintains that the collection of Hadith by al-Bukari contains 199 references to the word jihad and, as she emphatically points out, "every one using the term to mean warfare against infidels."[41] An expression of this form of jihad is seen through the account of the Battle of Badr, which gives evidence to Muhammad's first victory; however, more important to this discussion, his first militant action for the "cause" as well. Additionally, prominence for Muslims is tied to this battle as credit for the victory is seen as the result of divine intervention on the part of Allah. The reason for this is due to Muhammad's compliment of men were reportedly quite outnumbered and, given these odds, would not have been expected to win. This "miraculous event,"[42] in turn, substantiates the Islamists grounds and serves as a unifying rallying point. Another example would be Osama bin Laden's declaration of jihad against the U.S. bringing the fight to American soil, in spite of bin Laden's claims purporting the actions as being defensive in nature.

So, given these examples, what serves as the paramount take away? For the intent of this paper, the central focus is not on any aspects of turbidity or contradiction between the two forms, but on the critical, common denominator which mitigates any potential tensions between them – Islam and its religious goals. Cook points out, "Jihad does not detract from the fundamental goals of the religion, nor does it in any way contradict Islam. It regulates the relationship between Muslims and non-Muslims."[43] Furthermore, Ware offers that "Certainly it cannot be denied that radical Islamism extends its appeal to the universal Muslim community and in that sense it is a transnational phenomenon."[44] As such, the evidence appears clear that, "it is to religion, however misused or abused, that the jihadists regularly appeal when talking about their beliefs or explaining their actions."[45] Therefore, an effort to bridge the past of Islam and the employment of jihad as an obligatory charge to its followers, serves as the main tenant of the next block. Additionally, the dialogue addresses the radical Islamist of today and what can be learned from their words and actions prior to moving into a discussion on the relevance of all this to today's fight and American/Western counter efforts.

In speaking of today's brand of radical Islamist, many have asserted that the latest call to jihad first rang out twenty-five to thirty years ago. This period goes back to the late 1970s, early 1980s when the Soviets sought to increase their interests and establish a gateway to the Indian Ocean and looked to accomplish such through the establishment of a pro-Soviet government in Afghanistan. Unfortunately for them, a group of Muslim fundamentalists called the Mujahideen already controlled most of the country.[46] It should be noted that Mujahideen means those who struggle, with its root stemming from the term jihad. Additionally, two key points need mentioned at this juncture. The first centers on the fact that the historical record has shown the Soviets entered this war under the false assumption that their highly trained, well equipped Soviet force would simply prove to be too much for the guerilla-type, unconventional fighters, the Mujahideen insurgents employed. And, the second point attests to the Soviets' shortcoming in acknowledging the role religion played in their adversary's intent of actions. For regardless of the political differences dividing the groups making up the Mujahideen, "they were all united by a common religion that provided a motivation to fight and resist even more powerful than any political ideology,"[47] particularly atheist communism.

Why any of this is relevant relates to the fact that during this time an individual named Osama bin Laden moved to Afghanistan to pick up the fight along-side the Mujahideen and, in 1988, is credited with establishing *al Qaeda* or "The Base," which was, at that time, to serve as a central coordinating entity as part of the Afghan resistance movement. Additionally of relevance is that Ayman al-Zawahiri became bin Laden's ideological/theological mentor during this time.[48] Pertaining to this, it is said that Zawahiri, who ascribes to the lesser or offensive form of jihad, credits Qutb with giving rise to the contemporary jihadist movement. As for Qutb, he is recognized as the founder of the radical Islamist group known as the Society of Muslim Brothers in Egypt and is quoted as stating, "The cause of Islamic jihad should be sought in the very nature of Islam, and its [universal] role in the world."[49] Furthermore, Gerges relays, "Qutb popularized and legitimized the idea of making jihad a personal and permanent endeavor to confront jahili or non-Muslim leadership and society alike."[50] Accordingly, the impact these imputations had from Qutb to Zawahiri, and then from Zawahiri to bin Laden equally display themselves through the radical interpretations of Islamic tenants that eventually manifest themselves in such a way as to find justification in the use of, not only jihad, but more specifically through the use of terrorism as a tactic against an enemy of the faith, but also through the use of suicide attacks in pursuit of the greater cause. Moreover, these tactics were employed against both non-Muslim and eventually Muslims alike. Such actions, albeit seemingly doctrinally contradictory to the stated religious base, gets expressed as aspects of self-defense, which in turn shapes such actions as being mandatory under jihad and therefore, morally commendable.[51] The bottom-line of all this is, as previously iterated, a justified end - the establishment of an Islamic state through violence.

Since the Russian/Afghan war the world has witnessed a number of events/actions that have solidified this "new" jihadist manifesto from the first bombing of the World Trade Center in 1993, to the attacks/bombings of Khobar Towers, the U.S. Embassies in Tanzania and Kenya, and the USS Cole in 1996, 1998, and 2000 respectively. And certainly not least was the example witnessed on 11 September 2001 when the World Trade Center, the Pentagon, and Flight 93 were attacked. It was also within this timeframe, September 1996 that, bin Laden declared jihad against America. However, in regards to the latter event, the U.S. was not the only target of bin Laden's war, for he determined it would be a two front conflict. These fronts have been termed the near and the far wars. In regards to the near war, the terminology represents a "betrayal from within."[52] More specifically, bin Laden contended that Saudi Arabia's leaders, the royal family, had betrayed their ties to the Islamic community and must be overthrown. On the other end of bin Laden's spectrum of conflict, is the far war in which bin Laden seeks the downfall of the West and voiced his claims against Islam by arguing for the liberation of Islamic holy sites and the mandate requiring the departure of Western forces from the Arabian peninsula.[53] While the latter actions reflect a sentiment reminiscent of the Muslims during the Crusades, it is further

14

reasoned that bin Laden's jihad relates to the perceived U.S. betrayal of the Mujahideen in Afghanistan and American support for Israel. As Scheuer relays, according to bin Laden, these actions, viewed as "crimes and sins," are a "clear declaration of war on God, his messenger, and Muslims."[54] Scheuer adds that bin Laden also stated, "We believe that this [jihad] is a form of worship."[55] In both instances, the linkages are again clearly expressed between jihad and Islam; there is no separation of religion between Islam and an Islamist, only an added political slant. What is also clear is the fact that today's jihadist, most notably bin Laden and al Qaeda care not to distinguish between greater and lesser forms of jihad, for regardless of the reality of the situation, their intent is to create a defensive spin that will be used to foster support internal to the Muslim community, thus increasing its base. This increase of base through the winning over of the populace serves as the next transition point in this discussion.

The Nature of Today's Fight

Having established the foundational premise behind the argument for the need to address both religion and follower, the next several sections seek to address the type of conflict that has resulted, America's counter strategy, and conclude with what needs to be changed to most effectively achieve U.S. established ends. Clausewitz stated, "…the most far-reaching act of judgment that a statesman and commander have to make is [rightly to understand] the kind of war on which they are embarking…"[56] As such, what type of conflict is the War on Terror? For the purposes of this argument, the U.S. finds itself engaged in a global insurgency sponsored by terrorists who employ irregular warfare tactics. In support of this assertion, two more key terms need defining. Beginning with insurgency, Joint Publication (JP) 1-02 defines an insurgency as "an organized movement aimed at the overthrow of a constituted government through the use of subversion and armed conflict."[57] The second term, irregular warfare (IW), as defined by Air

15

Force Doctrine Document 2-3, is "a violent struggle among state and non-state actors for legitimacy and influence over the relevant populations."[58]

The reason these two terms along with terrorism, as defined previously, are required here stems from the fact that the current struggle is broad in scope and no one definition, to date, accurately or adequately captures its true breadth.[59] This is seen by looking at the full spectrum of the current operations. These radicals use subversion and armed conflict as their means of aggression; however, they are not necessarily organized into a single, interwoven network of movements. Additionally, it would be difficult to state that their intent is to overthrow a single constituted government, for their true objective is the downfall of the entire Western mindset and political structure. Likewise, this foe is comprised of a group of non-state actors who violently struggle against recognized states.[60] And lastly, their legitimacy is holistically based on the pursuit of religious/ideological goals premised on the use of violence and fear. Having said this, America's efforts in confronting this irregular, terrorist enemy must shift from the typical American, conventional, state-on-state style of warfare and transform itself into one which can evolve on demand, affording greater recognition of a much broader coverage in relation to today's myriad of military and paramilitary operations. Operations that may, by their very nature, carry forward and cover an extended period of time.[61]

Subscribing then to the position that the U.S. involvement in its war on terror does indeed conform with a hybridization of these definitions articulated for an insurgency, IW, and terrorism, what key aspects of the enemy's course of action prove imperative to recognize in advance to developing an effective counter to the resultant threat? The response to this question involves looking at two conditions which have been shown to be instrumental for the conduct of a successful insurgency as articulated by the influential French military officer and scholar David

16

Galula. As Galula enounced, the first basic requirement for an insurgency to succeed relates to having an appealing cause. Accordingly, there are three key components that lend themselves to such success. The first pertains to the need for the cause to be attractive to the largest number of supporters, while minimizing the number of opponents. Secondly, the insurgent must be able to identify himself totally with the cause or with the targeted population attracted by it. And lastly, a successful cause is one that takes on deep roots within its supporters, thus fostering staying power or longevity.[62]

If one transposes these keys to the War on Terror, one recognizes that the Islamists of today believe Islam is the one true faith that will dominate not only the Arab community, but the whole globe, as well as see their cause as integral in bringing this all-encompassing Islamic state to fruition. Extrapolating further, this cause finds an affinity with the whole of the estimated 1.5 billion-plus Muslims of the world, not just a small percentage of extremists. Furthermore, Islam, as highlighted earlier, is the youngest of the three monotheistic world religions. Not with standing, it has developed very deep roots over its 1,400 year history. These roots are expressed socially, when an action is perceived to exploit Muslims by non-Muslims. Additionally, "the cause" takes root economically through the voicing of exploitation of the West against the Arab world and its vast oil reserves. It also expresses itself religiously and culturally as a Muslim/Arab cause battling against perceived Western/Secular domination. And lastly, it finds further expression as an artificial cause by the exploitation of history and the fall of a once great Arab society.[63] Therefore, based on said factors, the evidence would appear to support the position that the enemy has got it right when it comes to the first key measure of an insurgency – an attractive cause.

Likewise, the insurgents hit the mark when looking at the second canon for a successful insurgency as described by Galula that being the counter insurgent must present or possess a police and administrative weakness in its camp. Relative to the conflict under review, this factor is evidenced by the insurgents' wanton use of terrorism to bring an elevated awareness to their cause. How this applies relates to the fact that the world, particularly the West displays a weak constitution for such action. In turn, it offers a point of weakness of which the insurgent can exploit. Furthermore, as witnessed, "if the problem is merely latent, the first task of the insurgent is to make it acute by raising the political consciousness of the masses. Terrorism may be a quick means of producing this effect."[64] The fact that jihadists overtly use such a strategy to bring light to and further their cause is no secret. In turn, U.S. National Strategy for Combating Terrorism acknowledges such and established a dualistic approach that expresses America's vision for the battle which rests first on "The defeat of violent extremism as a threat to our way of life as a free and open society;" while the second premise recommends, "The creation of a global environment inhospitable to violent extremists and all who support them."[65]

Tangentially, while this strategy highlights a myriad of concepts that do not give rise to terrorism, it also speaks to those that do, to include describing it as "an ideology that justifies murder."[66] The pivotal shortcoming with the latter premise lies with the conclusion that this ideology appeals to the "deliberate killing of innocents."[67] As previously argued, jihad takes this argument away in that it enables the justification of all in the attainment of the religious-based ends, of which tie directly back to the foundational elements Islam rests upon. Therefore, in order to serve as viable expressions of a desired end state, the vision must translate into an appropriate strategical object, which in turn will be used to direct American counter efforts, both of which are focused on next.

American Counter Efforts

So what is a strategical object; what should such be in relation to America's war on terror; and, how does it aid in the refinement of focus of American counter efforts? In response to the first question, a strategical object of war can be thought of as "the destruction of the enemy's fighting strength."[68] Military doctrine adds to this definition and describes a strategical object as any physical or moral entities that are the primary components of physical or moral strength, power, and resistance and refers to such as a center of gravity (COG).[69] Additionally, Dr. Joe Strange appends to the description by stating that a COG does not only contribute to strength, it is the strength,[70] it is the aspect of the enemy most guarded against. As such, the center of gravity in this scenario is clearly Islam, as it is the centerpiece of all actions conducted by the Islamists.

With the source of the adversary's power established, it only makes sense that such would serve as the focus of any counter strategy. Likewise, along with such identification, it would make additional sense to seek out an area of weakness or what is known as a critical vulnerability (CV) to attack. As Reilly defines it, a CV is an "aspect or component of the adversary's capability that when deficient will create decisive effects against the enemy's COG."[71] In other words, this CV would serve as the focus in any effort to mitigate or negate the adversary's source of strength. Accordingly, the contention that Islam is a moderate, non-violent religion serves as a key vulnerability to the enemy's capacity to foster and propagate their cause. As such, these two elements sync up and lend support to do additional assessment which seeks out the identification of a point or spot for attack. This locale affords the attacker (the U.S./West), a greater advantage relative to its effort to defeat the enemy (the radical Islamist). The key for America in all this is the object of any counter strategy must account for the enemy's

19

source of strength. In doing so, a critical point of weakness needs identified in order to focus effort. An example would be if the U.S. and Western Allies could foster such a world-wide accepted moderation of Islamic doctrine, the radical Islamists would lose footing in their attempts to arouse negative sentiment and hostilities against the West.

In acceptance of the position that the War on Terror is a global insurgency in which the enemy has successfully met the two stated critical attributes tied to successful operations and the realization that in planning to counter said operations a point of weakness must be identified (moderate Muslim populace) in order to effectively counter the adversary's source of strength (Islam), the way ahead for U.S. counter measures must begin with the devising of a new, comprehensive strategy. This strategy must account for both enemy motivation and behavior. Along this vein, two precepts associated with a successful counterinsurgency strategy are offered. The first law states the population becomes the objective for the counterinsurgent, as it is for the insurgent. General Curtis Lemay stated when speaking on COIN type conflicts, "The task is to destroy the effectiveness of the insurgent's efforts and his ability to use the population for his own ends."[72] Therefore, a key enabler to achieve success is to realize that an effective counter strategy must include the allocation of not only the military, but it also must take into account and include political, economic, and other resources to most effectively attain the end goal – winning the hearts and minds of the population. Regarding this scenario, this equates to the Arab, Islamic peoples. Supporting this contention, Nagl, a respected expert on COIN relates, "Undue focus on military action clouds the key political realities, which can result in a military-dominated campaign plan that misses the real focus of an insurgency."[73] Stated differently, in a counterinsurgency, the final political goal most always takes precedent. In fact, although netting near-term gains, the use of military force might actually serve in a counterproductive manner relative to garnering the public's disposition towards the desired ends. Accordingly, Hart states, "For the spirit of barbarism can be weakened only during cessation of hostilities; war strengthens it – pouring fuel on the flames."[74] Along these lines, for a COIN operation to succeed, simultaneous governmental reforms, education, information operations, and economic programs need executed to enhance, compliment, and possibly supplant the primacy of military intervention.[75] All these initiatives contribute to the resonating of an intent of turning the people away from the enemy's cause and over to yours. Lastly, again referring to Nagl's expertise on the matter of COIN, he also adds "the indirect approach to defeating an insurgency by focusing on dividing the people from the insurgents, removing the support that they require to challenge the government effectively, is rather different from the direct approach [using military means] and in the long term is usually more effective."[76] The bottom-line then is, for America to defeat radical Islamism; a moderate base of believers must be supported to counter the militant voice within the Muslim populace.

Aligning closely with the first edict, the second law emphasizes that support is gained through an active minority. Relayed another way, trust and allegiance of the populace is gained by placing a priority on "winning the support of the population rather than defeating the insurgents, thus separating the insurgents from their source of supply and recruits in the population."[77] The imperative with both positions is that the people must embrace defeating the subversion. In this case, the perversion of Islam is found as that priority. Additionally, when speaking of establishing priorities/objectives, it must be remembered that "victory is not only the destruction in a given area of the insurgent's forces and his political organization," as Galula relays, "it is also the permanent isolation of the insurgent from the population, isolation not enforced upon the population but maintained by and with the population."[78]

So, with all this said, if victory is then determined not by the combatants, but by the "spectators," what must be done to win over this third party's hearts and minds? A good first step would be to move outside of the Western/Secular frame of reference and obtain a more comprehensive understanding of Arab culture, ideologies, and religion. The reason an Arab worldview is chosen over a more refined Muslim worldview stems from the fact that although religion serves as the central factor to this discussion, it is not the sole factor. More specifically, by defining worldview as "a culture's orientation toward God, humanity, nature, questions of existence, the universe and cosmos, life, and moral and ethical reasoning, suffering, death and other philosophical issues that influence how its members perceive their world"[79] a depiction of the complexity and myriad of enablers that impact and mold persons of a given culture begins to show itself. Additionally, it must be realized that these factors overlap. Furthermore, one factor truly cannot be thought about in isolation of the others. Two examples pertain to history and language. In regards to language, although Islam, a major player in the Arab/Middle Eastern world has a history going back approximately 1400 years, while Arab history extends back in time several thousand more years. In turn, many believers of Islam also have a concurrent historical heritage that resonates just as loudly, if not more loudly than their religious ties. A second example is language with Arabic being looked at as the original and official language of the Qur'an. However, an Arab, or any person who speaks Arabic, is not a guarantee to being a Muslim, for there are also sizeable populations of Christian and Jewish Arabs. As such, an understanding of the impact such factors as a language, culture, and history hold provides direct relevance in association with the transcending role religion plays across the Arab community and should be considered when seeking an understanding of, not only the militant Islamists, but also those they seek to dissuade to their cause, the non-militant Arab populace, both Muslim and non-Muslim alike.

Along these lines there are a number of conceptual differences that must be understood within the context of the Arab worldview. While Westerners typically view a cause and effect linkage between events, thus unifying the two together, Arabs, on the other hand have a more atomistic outlook in which they "see the world and events as isolated incidents, snapshots, and particular moments in time."[80] A second difference aligns to the fact that a large percentage of Arabs view religion/faith as being central to life. Reiterating from the section on Islam, Muslim Arabs believe their lives are controlled by a divine source. On the flip side of this, the West adheres to a more prominent voice in which belief centers on personal choice. This extends to the concept of fatalism which describes an Arab perspective in which the individual believes life is controlled by the will of God, and, in turn, places their future outside of their control.[81] Contrary to this is how the Western mindset looks at the individual as being in control of their life and can then act accordingly to direct events that determine their future. Additionally, where the West voices concern over a separation of church and state along with the rights of the individual, Arab governments have a distinctive focus on religion, albeit with some countries more central than others. Furthermore, family for the Arab populace is considered foremost on the community and is a tight-knit group with the father as head, while for the West there is a much greater emphasis on the self, with much more acceptance of unit fragmentation. Along with family is the concept of honor. For an Arab, family honor is more important than the individual[82] and is to be defended at all costs, whereas, this is not the case for the large part of the Western world. As relayed, these concepts, of which there are a number more, reflect the importance of not only understanding the nature of the conflict, but also, the nature of all the actors involved.

Summarizing this contention is the famous Chinese military strategist Sun Tzu who stated, "Know thy enemy, know yourself, your victory will never be endangered."[83] Relative to this global insurgency, this statement must now include "know thy spectators" as well.

A second deviation from what has shown itself to be the norm during this war is to ensure a comprehensive strategy is devised upfront as compared to one generated piecemeal as the conflict unfolds. On this front, its aim should be as Hart relayed, "to produce a decision without any serious fighting."[84] In revisiting the point made previously regarding the nature of this conflict, this strategy must shift away from the conventional, sport of kings-type adherence to one with a more fluid battle space in which a decisive battle is likely not to be encountered. Accordingly, a victory won't be total or complete, nor won on behalf of another. Regarding this last point Walzer describes this as a characteristic need for ownership of action and self-determination. He specifically relays, "The (internal) freedom of a political community can be won only by the member of that community."[85] For the context of the War on Terror, this extends to the whole, both Arab and Western communities functioning as the global actors involved.

Along those lines, this means the West must discontinue of any preferential treatment towards the Arab community under the banner of accommodation and out of a sense of fear resulting from the overt, in-your-face, violence perpetrated by the militants. This type of accommodation is witnessed in a number of ways, whether it be the attempted use of public monies to satisfy Muslim religious requirements, when the same measures would not be acceptable under similar circumstances for a different religion or political group, to the pursuit of charges against a film maker for perceived insults resulting from overlaying Qur'anic verses with footage of violence when the freedom of speech typically trumps such charges, to standing by as an individual is killed over their artistic depiction and expression of the prophet Muhammad, to a publishing firm refusing to sponsor a book due to the potential negative response on the part of these extremists/radicals. The intent of these examples is not to minimize perceptions, but to relay that although there are clear differences between individuals, nations, and cultures amongst the spectators of this conflict, both sides must acknowledge, accept, and capitalize on the differences, for "vitality springs from diversity – which makes for real progress so long as there is mutual toleration, based on the recognition that worse may come from attempts to suppress differences rather than from acceptance of them."[86] Lastly, relaying the sentiment of Gabriel, America can no longer stand back deaf, blind, and mute to the evil that is against us [the West]. We must become engaged and make it all of our business to echo the dictum that "all men are created equal; that they are endowed by their Creator with certain unalienable rights; that among these are life, liberty, and the pursuit of happiness."[87] As to whether these rights are dictated by sharia directive may be for the Muslim community to decide internal to itself; however, it should never be at the expense of western progress and standards, for the spread of democracy may not be the answer for all, but the expectation should not be the sacrifice of it either.

On the other side of this premise is the moderate Muslim voice, which has unfortunately been largely missing from the public scene. For this community, it can no longer sit back and quietly acquiesce to the militant extremists' actions and banter. Their leaders must step forward and renounce the violence; and the actions of anti-Western sentiment. For progress to be had the silence must be broken, for anything short must be perceived as acceptance. Simply, actions must display beyond any doubt as to their intentions of either being with the West, committed against this foe, or not, there truly is no middle ground.

Lastly, while the previous two points expressed strategic objectives in broad, general terms. This last section seeks to posit a number of specific actions that could be taken to better posture America in swaying the sentiment of the spectators. The points of discussion come from a prominent al Qaeda leader, Abu Yahya al-Libi who offered the following six tips to wage ideological warfare: highlight the views of jihadist who renounce violence; publicize stories about jihadist atrocities against Muslims; enlist Muslim religious leaders to denounce jihadists as heretics; back Islamic movements that emphasize politics over jihad; discredit and neutralize jihadist ideologues; and, play up personal or doctrinal disputes among jihadist.[88]

Starting with highlighting the views of jihadists who renounce violence, such views tie into the previous section. It serves a number of purposes to include a dissenting voice; a voice to thoughts and perspectives that, possibly out of fear of reprisal, may have previously been silent. This voice may also function as a source of support and/or motivation that might spawn other like-minded spectators to begin to speak out against and challenge the militants' actions and position. Additionally, it shows which side one supports, thus opening opportunities for outreach on the part of the counterinsurgent. Regarding publicizing stories about jihadist atrocities against Muslims, stories addressing like actions against non-Muslims need added as well. With this, the public, both Western and non-Western, must be confronted with the harsh reality of the enemy, particularly in America. The press must be willing to display the horrendous and graphic nature of this conflict with an open, in-the-face starkness that uncovers its brutality first hand. Beheadings and other acts of violence need broadcasted on American television; stories depicting the savagery must be unveiled. The bottom-line intent of this is to create a sense of humanity through the expression of the in-humane actions of the enemy and to reveal the reality that as the West seeks to express itself as tolerant in hopes of a like reciprocation, this adversary takes the inch given in the name of accommodation under the banner of conquest.[89]

The next four suggestions go together under a religious umbrella of action. Three of these directly relate together starting with the requirement for the West to develop a cadre of moderate Muslim religious leaders willing and capable of denouncing the jihadists' using the very same Islamic doctrine they use to justify their atrocities. However, based on the potential for such individuals to be perceived as being under Western influence and, thus, lacking sufficient credibility, a grassroots effort within the non-Western Muslim community must pick up this mantle and bring forth a loud, clear, and definitive voice to the resident Muslim populace who profess the moderate religion they contend Islam actually is. The bottom-line being, if there is a moderate voice amongst the core Muslim community, it must be vocal in its objection of the high-jacking of their religion. They must openly deface any distortions to Islamic text and right align any misinterpretations of the same. By doing so they fulfill two more prescribed actions, those being discrediting and neutralizing jihadist ideologues and playing up personal or doctrinal disputes among jihadists. For it is through their willingness to bring forth and substantiate charges of heresy on the part of the Islamists, not to mention to discredit their position and erode their cause.

The fourth action that should be taken is for the West to back Islamic movements that emphasize politics over jihad. Such a movement does not necessarily align with the often referred to Pan-Arabic manifestation in which, as Lewis describes, all Arab nations are "united in a common polity," but possibly one in which the Arab world would be linked by a common language, culture, religion, history, and destiny.[90] This means that some degree of separation is created between church and state, a secularization of sorts. While still allowing for religion to play a role in government, the focus would be outside the vein of establishing a sharia-driven caliphate, again mitigating the enemy's source of strength. The resultant commonality would be looked towards to take responsibility for their own affairs, thus seeking the means to root out and counter the factors behind the radical Islamist efforts that create the unacceptable state of stagnation, if not regression, currently witnessed in varying degrees by the affected states. The bottom-line behind all these actions can be summarized by the old adage that relays that a house divided cannot stand. Once in such a fragile, disjointed state, the West can look to capture the required support of the Arab/Muslim spectators and seize the upper hand.

Lastly, when speaking of these six to-dos, they must be thought of with a mindset seeking information dominance, particularly through the use of offensive information operations (IO). JP 3-13 defines offensive IO as "The integrated use of assigned and supporting capabilities and activities, mutually supported by intelligence, to affect adversary decision-makers."[91] Through its employment, offensive IO operations target the human decision-maker.[92] Why this is important stems from the fact that one of the difficulties of fighting an insurgency is that the enemy can be seen as being everywhere as well as being nowhere. Carrying this into the 21st Century and the increased reliance on media and the electromagnetic spectrum to conduct operations, superiority must be obtained if the West has any hope of gaining sway over the spectators. Thomas adds emphasis to this sentiment as he relayed, "While they continue to focus on physical and barbaric actions that induce terror, today's insurgents are also savvy and informed. They are adept at using Internet information and other media sources against us..."[93] He goes on to say, "the Internet can offer a kinder face for the insurgent, or it can offer harsh reality (beheading of an individual) for those who choose to support the 'infidels.'"[94] This use of propaganda thus offers an allusive medium in which the insurgent can not only increase its base, but simultaneously subvert the efforts of the counterinsurgency. As the former Chairman of the Joint Chiefs of Staff, General Richard B. Myers, has stated, "This is a new kind of war. The military may not be decisive."[95] In turn, the West must quickly adapt and seek out a more holistic governmental approach to defeating it; an approach that incorporates the full spectrum of instruments of national power, not just that of the military. This sentiment gains credence when supported by the words of the former Commander of U.S. Central Command, General Tommy Franks who relayed, "To maintain information dominance, we must commit to improving our ability to influence target audiences and manipulate our adversary's information environment. Continued development of these capabilities is essential."[96] In regards to the former, a significantly emotional appeal must be devised; one which counters the often inherently suspicious nature of the Arab world toward the Western worldview. It should address concepts of importance such as honor, faith, justice, and equality. Along this vein, the strategy must be perceived as legitimate and represent a unifying cause reflecting a vision for the masses. In summation of this premise, in an age where information is what makes the world go around. The entity that gains supremacy and control of it will be the one to succeed in winning not only the information war, but the war of the mind, and, in turn, the war on terror.

Summary and Conclusion

In response to the question as to why these radical Islamists perpetrate the violence they do, Bridgette Gabriel offers a succinct response, "Because they hate."[97] She continues by adding that "They hate our way of life. They hate our freedom. They hate our democracy. They hate the practice of every religion but their own."[98] As this paper has shown, this latter statement serves as the crux of the matter when arguing for a changed strategy relative to countering this threat. For the case made contends this "hate" clearly revolves around the adversary's belief that there is no god but their god and that they are mandated to spread their faith, even through the use of violence. This militant religious fervor then seeks to, as Ware argues, mobilize sentiment towards the goal (the destruction of the Western world-view) and by so doing cross the boundary into political ideology, at least in the contemporary sense of the word.[99] Understanding this, one can more fully grasp what was meant by Clausewitz who wrote, "If we keep in mind that war springs from some political purpose, it is natural that the prime cause of its existence will remain the supreme consideration in conducting it..."[100] Therefore, under the premise that the jihadis "cause" focuses on Islam, Islam then must serve as the supreme consideration as the West, particularly the U.S., seeks to devise effective counter strategies against this foe's global insurgent efforts. In conclusion, in order to eliminate or at least mitigate the effects of these radical Islamist insurgents a counter revolution by, not only the moderate Muslims, but by all opposition to such murderous ideology must begin. To do so, America's and the West's strategy must therefore begin to not only focus on those who hate, but more so on what those who hate love – Islam.

[1] Lamont, James Joule

[2] Fuller, ACSC Red Course Book, p.76

[3] President, NSS, p. i

[4] Ibid, p. 9

[5] Habeck, Knowing the Enemy, p. 13

[6] Snodgrass, Know Your Enemy, pp. 31

[7] Darley, Strategic Imperative, p. 5

[8] President, Combating Terrorism, p.7

[9] Zartman, ACSC Blue Course Book, p. 98

[10] Ibid, p. 98

[11] Dept of State, Patterns of Global Terrorism

[12] Lippman, Understanding Islam, p. 2

[13] Ibid, p. 4

[14] Caner, Unveiling Islam, p. 55

[15] Cook, Understanding Jihad, p. 5

[16] Caner, Unveiling Islam, p. 47

[17] Lippman, Understanding Islam, p. 5

[18] Caner, Unveiling Islam, p. 31

[19] Koran, p. 76

[20] Ibid, p. 98

[21] Ibid, p. 210

[22] Cook, Understanding Islam, p. 21

[23] Lewis, The Crisis of Islam, p. 7

[24] Cook, Understanding Islam, p. 6

[25] Caner, Unveiling Islam, p. 48

[26] Koran, p. 57

[27] Ibid, p. 207

[28] Cook, Understanding Islam, p. 19

[29] Habeck, Knowing the Enemy, p. 17

[30] Ibid, p. 4

[31] Baker, The Cultural Heritage of Arabs, p. 136

[32] Gabriel, Because They Hate, p. 149

[33] Koran, p. 53

[34] Ibid, p.54

[35] Habeck, Knowing the Enemy, p. 20

[36] Lippman, Understanding Islam, p. 111

[37] Habeck, Knowing the Enemy, p. 20

[38] Ibid, p. 116

[39] Lewis, The Crisis of Islam, p. 33

[40] Cook, Understanding Islam, p. 43

[41] Gabriel, Because They Hate, p. 149

[42] Cook, Understanding Islam, p. 30

[43] Ibid, p. 104

[44] Ware, A Radical Islamist Concept of Conflict, p. 29

[45] Habeck, Knowing the Enemy, p. 18

[46] Corum, Small Wars, p. 389

[47] Ibid, p. 395

[48] Zartman, ACSC Blue Course Book, p. 101

[49] Gerges, The Far Enemy, pp. 4-5

[50] Ibid, p. 9

[51] Ware, A Radical Islamist Concept of Conflict, p. 42

[52] Scheuer, ACSC Blue Course Book, p. 124

[53] Zartman, ACSC Blue Course Book, p. 102

[54] Scheuer, ACSC Blue Course Book, p. 126

[55] Ibid, p. 132

[56] Clausewitz, On War, pp. 88-89

[57] JP 1-02, DoD Dictionary, p. 268

[58] AFDD 2-3, Irregular Warfare, p. 2

[59] Military Review, Redefining Insurgency, p. 117

[60] Ibid, p. 117

[61] AFCC 2-3, Irregular Warfare, p. 2

[62] Galula, Counterinsurgency Warfare, p. 13

[63] Ibid, p. 15

[64] Ibid, p. 15

[65] President, Combating Terrorism, p 7

[66] Ibid, p. 10

[67] Ibid, p. 10

[68] Fuller, ACSC Red Course Book, p. 72

[69] JP 5-0, Joint Operation Planning, p. IV-8

[70] Strange, ACSC Purple Course Book, p. 45

[71] Reilly, Operational Design, p. 23

[72] AFDD, Irregular Warfare, p. vi

[73] Nagl, Learning to Eat Soup with a Knife, p. 26

[74] Hart, ACSC Red Course Book, p. 101

[75] Corum, Small Wars, p. 426

[76] Nagl, Learning to Eat Soup with a Knife, p. 28

[77] Ibid, p72

[78] Galula, Counterinsurgency Warfare, p. 54

[79] Samovar, Communication Between Cultures, p.73

[80] Ibid, p. 13

[81] ACSC, Arab Culture Elective

[82] Ibid, p. 13

[83] Sun Tzu, The Art of War, p. 129

[84] Hart, ACSC Red Course Book, p. 83

[85] Walzer, Just and Unjust Wars, p. 88

[86] Hart, ACSC Red Course Book, p. 98

[87] Gabriel, Because They Hate, p. 185

[88] Economist, Leaders: How to win the war within Islam,

[89] Jeremiah, What in the World is Going On, p.83

[90] Lewis, Rethinking the Middle East, p.101

[91] JP 3-13, Information Operations, p. GL-9

[92] Information Operations, p. 112

[93] Thomas, Cyber Silhouettes, p. 47

[94] Ibid, p. 53

[95] Ibid, p. 160

[96] Ibid, p. 159

[97] Gabriel, Because They Hate, p. 145

[98] Ibid, p. 145

[99] Ware, A Radical Islamist Concept of Conflict, p. 39

[100] Clausewitz, On War, p. 87

Bibliography

Ann Lamont, "James Joule: The Great Experimentere Who Was Guided by God,"
http://www.answersingenesis.org/creation/v15/i2/joule.asp

Baker, William G. *The Cultural Heritage of Arabs, Islam, and the Middle East.* Dallas, TX:
Brown Books Publishing, 2003.

Cook, David. *Understanding Jihad.* Los Angles, California Berkley: University of California
Press, 2005.

Corum, James S., and Johnson, Wray R. *Airpower in Small Wars.* Lawrence, Kansas:
University Press of Kansas, 2003.

Darley, Col William M. "Strategic Imperative: The Necessity for Values Operations as
Opposed to Information Operations in Iraq and Afghanistan." *Air and Space Power Journal*
(Spring 2007).
http://www.airpower.maxwell.af.mil/airchornicles/apj/apj07/spr07/darleyspr07.html
(accessed 18 October 2008).

Department of State, Patterns of Global Terrorism,
http://www.state.gov/s/ct/rls/crt/2000/2419.htm

Economist, "Leaders: How to Win the War Within Islam; Al Qaeda's Global Jihad,"
http://proquest.umi.com/pgdweb

Fuller, J.F.C. "Strategical Paralysis as the Object of the Decisive Attack." In *Applied Warfare
Course* coursebook, edited by Sharon McBride, 73-80. Maxwell AFB, AL: Air University
Press, October 2008.

Gabriel, Brigitte. *Because They Hate.* New York, NY: St. Martin's Press, 2006.

Galula, David. *Counterinsurgency Warfare: Theory and Practice.* Westport, CT and London:
Praeger Publishers, 2006.

Gerges, Fawaz A. *The Far Enemy*: Why Jihad Went Global. New York: Cambridge University
Press, 2005.

Grapeshisha, "Information and Insight on the UAE," http://www.grapeshisha.com/arab-versus-
western-perspectives.html

Habeck, Mary. *Knowing the Enemy*: *Jihadist Ideology and the War on Terror.* New Haven: Yale
University Press, 2006

Hart, B.H. Liddell. *Strategy.* In *Applied Warfare Course* coursebook, edited by Sharon McBride,
81-101. Maxwell AFB, AL: Air University Press, October 2008.

Jeremiah, David, *What In The World Is Going On*, Nashville, TN: Thomas Nelson, Inc., 2008.

Joint Publication (JP) 1-02. *Department of Defense Dictionary of Military and Associated Terms.* 17 October 2008.

Joint Publication (JP) 3-13. *Information Operations.* In *Joint Forces* course book, edited by Sharon McBride, 99-106. Maxwell AFB, AL: Air University Press, July 2008.

Joint Publication (JP) 5-0. *Joint Operation Planning.* 26 December 2006.

Leigh Armistead, ed., Information Operation: Warfare and the Hard Reality of Soft Power, Dulles, NA: Potamac Books, 2004.

Lewis, Bernard. *The Crisis of Islam*: *How War and Unholy Terror*. New York: Random House Inc, 2003.

Lewis, Bernard. Rethinking the Middle East. *Foreign Affairs* 71, no. 4 (Fall 1992): 99-119.

Lippman, Thomas W. *Understanding Islam; An Introduction to the Muslim World.* New York: Penguin Putnam, 2002.

Nagl, John. *Learning to Eat Soup with a Knife: Counterinsurgency Lessons from Malaya and Vietnam.* Chicago, IL: University of Chicago Press, 2002.

Office of the President of the United States. *National Strategy for Combating Terrorism.* Washington, DC. September 2006.

Office of the President of the United States. *The National Security Strategy of the United States of America.* Washington, DC. March 2006.

Reilly, Jeffrey M. *Operational Design: Shaping Decision Analysis through Cognitive Vision.* Air Command and Staff College, Maxwell AFB, AL, October 2008.

Samovar, Larry A., Porter, Richard E., McDaniel, Edwin R, *Communication Between Cultures* (California: Thomson Learning, Inc., 2007).

Scheuer, Michael. "Getting to Know Bin Laden: Substantive Themes of the Jihad." In *InterNational Security Studies* coursebook, edited by Sharon McBride, 121-141. Maxwell AFB, AL: Air University Press, August 2008.

Snodgrass, Col Thomas E. "Know Your Enemy." *Air and Space Power Journal* 22, no. 3 (Fall 2008): 31-33. http://web.ebscohost.com (accessed 18 October 2008).

Strange, Joe, and Col Richard Iron. "Part 2: The CG-CC-CR-CV Construct: A Useful Tool to Understand and Analyze the Relationship Between Centers of Gravity and Their Critical Vulnerabilities." In *Joint Campaign Planning: Volume 6* course book, edited by Sharon

McBride, 41-56. Maxwell AFB, AL: Air University Press, January 2009.

Sun Tzu. *The Art of War*. Translated by Samuel B. Griffith. New York, NY and Oxford: Oxford
    University Press, 1963.

The Koran Interpreted. Translated by A.J. Arbury. New York: MacMillan, 1996.

Thomas, Timothy l. *Cyber Silhouettes: Shadows Over Information Operations*. Foreign
    Military Studies Office, Fort Leavenworth, KS, 2005.

U.S. Army Training and Doctrine Command, Arab Cultural Awareness: 58 Factsheets: Ft.
    Leavenworth, KS.

Walzer, Michael. *Just and Unjust Wars*. 4th ed. New York, NY: Basic Books, 1977.

Ware, Lew B., "A Radical Islamist Concept of Conflict", *Terrorism National Security Policy
and the Homefront*, 15 May 1995, U.S. Army War College, 28-50.

Zartman, Jonathan. "Historical Development of the Ideology of Al Qaeda (The Base)." In
    InterNational Security Studies coursebook, edited by Sharon McBride, 98-103. Maxwell
    AFB, AL: Air University Press, August 2008